THE

ABC'S

OF LIFE

BY BYRON V. GARRETT

LIFE WORKS INTERNATIONAL
CLINTON, MARYLAND

Life Works International
P.O. Box 2158
Clinton, Maryland 20735

Book and cover design by Cybis Communications. Lock crafted by T. & C. Latané.
Copy edited by Ryan Underwood and Gregory Booth.

ISBN 0-9755938-0-3

Printed in the United States of America
First Printing September 1995
Reprinting June 2008

ACKNOWLEDGEMENTS

To the ONE above who leads, guides and directs all that I do;

To my parents who serve as the compass for my ways and the foundation of my wisdom;

To my brothers (Frankie & Ronnie), my big sister (Evelyn Taylor) and sisters-in-law (Gerri & Sherry), thanks for your unwavering support and encouragement as I live my dreams;

And to my nephews – you are constant reminders of why I do what I do. I draw inspiration knowing that you have a great future ahead.

To all of my uncles, aunts, cousins, etc. thanks for always being there and having my back.

Kudos to my personal advisory board: Gregory Booth, Overseer & Lady Ransom, Ryan & Carrie Underwood, Genel Burwell, Doretta Thomas and Nicole Davis.

Special thanks to the Greater Progressive Church Family, TRI Leadership Resources, staff of the Governor's Office, ELAP Cohort at Pepperdine University, the staff, students and families of Progressive Leadership Academy and Progressive Junior High School, and those who have loved and supported me along the way.

My deepest appreciation to the tens of thousands of students, community leaders, parents, educators, and corporations who have used and lived the ABC's of LIFE. I take great pride in the work we have achieved together and look forward to seeing you at the next level.

INTRODUCTION

Greetings! You are embarking upon a journey to unlock your life and unleash the power of leadership, success and life management. I applaud your efforts. The first step towards being where you want to be in life is the recognition that there is somewhere you want to be. For each of us, we are obligated to determine, understand and identify our mission in life. I live by the personal mantra…you should find something in life that you love doing, you'd do it for free, but do it so well you get paid for it.

I've reached the conclusion that everyone in life is a success story. The mere fact that you are breathing makes you a success given the fact that people die every single day. Never take this simple reality for granted. To that end, you have a duty to yourself to make the most of your life so that you become a significant contribution. I like to make a distinction between being successful and being highly successful. Allow the ABC's to be your "how to" guide to living a HIGHLY successful life.

As you pursue your dreams, you will by no doubt encounter dream makers and dream busters. Dream busters are those who attempt to rain on your parade by striving to dissuade you from achieving your goals and living your life on purpose. I challenge you to seek dream makers – those who thrive in the midst of chaos. Dream makers are visionary change agents who see the world differently than most. When the world pushes them, they dig deep and push back. Dream makers do not accept the status quo and "no" is not part of their vocabulary. They live in the realm of possibility. The essence of a dream maker is the uncanny ability to see beyond present situations while transforming stumbling blocks into stepping-stones and obstacles into opportunities. You, my friend, are destined to live the life of a dream maker.

THE ABC's

OF LIFE

[fig. 1]

{Aa}

ACCEPT THE

ABC's OF LIFE

CHALLENGE

ACCEPT THE CHALLENGE

{Aa}

You must be willing to accept the challenge to be highly successful in life. People spend their entire life waiting for opportunity. They spend time waiting for great things to happen. Instead of waiting for opportunity, take hold of your future and face each day with a spirit of optimism and excitement. The adage, time waits for no one, is true. I remember my parents telling me as a child that the early bird gets the worm. This virtue still holds true…no matter your vocation or background, begin to accept the challenge as soon as the sun begins to rise.

As sure as the sun rises, you have 24 hours to accept the challenge. No time for second guessing yourself. You'll encounter hundreds of people throughout life who will second-guess you. Leave those minor details to those who live minor lives. You are on the verge of achieving greatness. Embrace it and make this your reality.

Accepting the challenge requires that you take action. Whether it's a baby step, a hop, a jump or a significant leap, begin each new day with the desire to excel and a passion for greatness. Without question, "accept" is an action word. You must accept the challenge, adopting the thought process that it's a brand new day. This new day is filled with opportunity disguised as obstacles. Know you are going to make it happen. Begin today- accept the challenge.

[fig. 2]

{Bb}

BELIEVE IN

ABC's of LIFE

YOURSELF

BELIEVE IN YOURSELF

{ B b }

During college, I took classes that dealt with non-profit management. One of the most important lessons I learned was the concept of finding a cause that you believe in with all your heart. My professor stated you must demonstrate your belief by giving to the cause. Highly effective people are those who operate in areas where they possess great belief.

A good salesperson believes in his or her product. While a great salesperson not only believes in the product but also exudes desire and purpose directly connected to the product for which they believe. To live a meaningful life, you must find one thing you believe in whole-heartedly. For parents, this may be creating a quality life for your family. For an athlete, this could be the belief in conditioning to excel in your sport. For teachers, this is probably the belief that all students can learn.

Whatever you believe in, recognize it's the belief in something bigger than you which keeps you going when you are tired, weary and worn down. This belief lifts you when others put you down and gives you the courage to try again when it appears you've fallen short. It's passionate belief that inspires others to believe as well.

You must believe in yourself. YOU are your primary cause. Unless you are strong and determined, you will have great difficulty getting others to believe in you. Believe in yourself.

[fig. 3]

{Cc}

CHOICE, NOT
DETERMINES

ABC's of LIFE

CHANCE,
SUCCESS

CHOICE, NOT CHANCE, DETERMINES SUCCESS

{ C c }

Success is all about the choices you make. Average people take chances. They waste time making excuses for what they have or have not done in life. You have the opportunity to live your life, as you'd like to. You have to take ownership of the decisions you make, good and bad. Stop making excuses like you have the "Shoulda-Coulda-Woulda" syndrome.

Shift your concentration from taking chances to making choices. Chances are something someone else gives you and are hard to count on. Choices, on the other hand, have no limit. Take ownership of your world with the understanding that you are the captain of your ship in the sea of life. If the boat sinks, it has nothing to do with your parents, employer, teachers, husband, wife, or children. In life, things may not have worked as you planned; yet you made the choice. You are only limited by your ability to think in the realm of possibility.

The ability to make excellent choices is the cornerstone of a highly successful person. Rather than dwell on bad choices I've made in the past, I focus on my future knowing that though I may have failed, I'm not a failure. Every time you look at your past, you are taking your eyes off your future. It's the choices you make, not the chances you take, which determines success in life.

[fig. 4]

{Dd}

DEVELOP YOUR
AND OBJECTI

ABC's OF LIFE

OWN GOALS
VES

DEVELOP YOUR OWN GOALS
AND OBJECTIVES
{Dd}

Living in today's society, you have the opportunity to dictate, determine and decide what happens in your life. Numerous factors have an impact on your life. When you get beyond age 18, life begins to operate differently. You move into an arena where you must develop your own goals and objectives. No longer can you rely upon others to lead, guide and direct you. You should begin positioning yourself to be a highly successful person.

Too often, you follow the directions your parents or teachers have set for you. You listen and follow the advice that others offer regarding life. To that end, you find yourself not where YOU want to be and begin making excuses and casting blame. If you are legally considered an adult, you have no right to blame anyone because this is your life.

What does or does not happen during your lifetime is completely at your discretion! If you do not know where you are going, any road will get you there. Begin today by writing down your 1-month, 1-year, 5-year and life long goals. Success does not happen over night, but it does happen over time. Begin to plot, plan and strategize for your future. Define yourself by developing your own goals and objectives. Remember, at the end of the day you are to be held accountable for your actions or lack thereof.

[fig. 5]

{Ee}

EXPECT FAILU
EXPECT SUCCE

ABC'S OF LIFE

RE, BUT ALSO

SS

EXPECT FAILURE, BUT ALSO EXPECT SUCCESS

{ E e }

There are times in life you must surrender to the reality that you have human limitations. Occasionally, we may try something over and over again only to be met with continued defeat and failure. Though I don't expect everything to be a failure, I do understand that in order to achieve greatly, I may fail greatly.

Give thought to the millions of people you know that know how to ride a bike. And out of those, only a small percentage hopped right on without training wheels and rode immediately. But if you are like me, you fell off time and time again. You don't know how to ride the bike because you fell off; you know how to ride because you got back on. Life is the same way, it's not a matter of failure, but rather it's discovering the power of getting back up to start again. Through practice you build the skill, ability and confidence to deliver when the key moment arises.

As you proceed through life, do not become discouraged at failure but look at it as a unique opportunity. Though I have failed often, it is during my failure that I have increased my knowledge, determination and perseverance to exceed even my own expectations. In other words, though you may have failed, rise with a spirit of determination combined with sheer will power, for you are a success waiting to happen.

[fig. 6]

{ Ff }

FIGHT ON, BE
FINISH WHAT

ABC's OF LIFE

FAITHFUL, AND YOU START

FIGHT ON, BE FAITHFUL, AND FINISH WHAT YOU START

{ F f }

Many people start things in life but never finish. I have great difficulty understanding why someone would start something and then lose sight of the goal. As we strive, we hope to accomplish great things but allow disappointments, setbacks, and maybe the pursuit of too many things to cloud our judgment. I refuse to allow others to deter me from my goal. When I'm centered on something, I am going to stick with it until my change comes.

I believe that an object in motion will continue in motion until acted upon by an opposite force. I know for a fact that the force of negativity is often greater than the force of positivity. Therefore you must work twice as hard and believe two times as much as anyone else to get to where it is you want to go. You have to fight the good fight, have faith in your abilities to deliver, and continue to strive until you finish what you start.

[fig. 7]

{Gg}

GRAVITATE TO

SUCCESSFUL

ABC'S OF LIFE

WARDS POSITIVE,
PEOPLE

GRAVITATE TOWARDS POSITIVE, SUCCESSFUL PEOPLE

{Gg}

I don't know how to put this; basically people suffer from "stinking thinking." Stinking thinking is the state of mind of a negative thinker. Their thinking process just plainly stinks. You may suffer from this thought process or it can be found in the people around you. Your challenge is to gravitate towards people who have a healthy, positive thought process.

As a boy, I was told that people could tell a lot about you by the company you keep. Who do you have around you? If they are not positive people who are about something, then you need to kick them to the curb. It doesn't matter if it is your mother/father, husband/wife, boss, neighbor, best friend – whomever, if they do not have a positive outlook on life – run! Literally, run in the other direction.

You need to surround yourself with people of like mind who are doing the things you strive and like to do. Do you know how great it would be to spend most of your time around people who think on a positive note? It will transform your life. You will be more vibrant, more energetic and more excited instead of being down in the dumps. Dumps are filled with garbage, which stinks. No time for stinking thinking. Resist getting caught up in the same old stuff again and again. Break the cycle by gravitating towards positive, successful people.

[fig. 8]

{Hh}

HARNESS EVERY

YOURSELF TO BE

ABC's of LIFE

THING WITHIN
HAPPY

HARNESS EVERYTHING WITHIN YOURSELF TO BE HAPPY
{Hh}

The ability to channel your energy, time and attention in the same direction is the premise of harnessing everything within you. Out of all that happens in life, no matter the situation or circumstance, you must harness all that you have to be focused. All too often we want the quick fix solutions and easy gains. Nothing in life worth having comes easy. Thus you have to stay committed and be determined to reach your goal.

I remember the film <u>The Karate Kid</u> where the martial arts teacher is striving to teach "Daniel-son" to protect himself. In the final round of the championship, Daniel-son sustains an injury and only has full use of one leg. As they start the round, the teacher says, "Daniel-son, focus." Within minutes Daniel-son uses his one leg in a crane motion to defeat his opponent. Son, daughter, mother, father, whatever it is you strive to do in life, focus! Harness the energy within to be successful.

Happiness is something money cannot afford. If it were, it would be traded on the New York Stock Exchange. Many squander their fortunes by buying "things" in hopes of attaining happiness. To find joy, peace and happiness you need to look inwards not outwards, beginning with yourself first, and not others. Harness everything within yourself to be happy.

[fig. 9]

{I i}

INITIATE THE

ABC's of LIFE

PROCESS

INITIATE THE PROCESS

{ I i }

Have you ever wondered why it seems some people get all the breaks and you are still struggling to just maintain? I would offer that they don't get all the breaks, but rather somewhere along the way they initiate the process. If you want to do better in school, on the job or in your community, you should continually seek those opportunities.

The word initiate requires you to take the first step. Instead of waiting for something to fall from the sky or waiting for all of the planets to align, you need to get your butt in motion. Why put off tomorrow that which you can do today? Initiate the process! You have the ability, the knowledge, the wisdom and the determination to do great things. Do yourself a favor - stop waiting for others to bestow good things upon you. Success doesn't come to you; you've got to go get it. Step out in faith and courage by making it happen TODAY. Yesterday is a memory and tomorrow is just a dream. You must initiate today to make tomorrow's dream a reality. In order to be someone you've never been, you must start doing things you've never done. Initiate the process – today is the first day of the rest of your life!

[fig. 10]

{ J j }

JEALOUSY GETS

ABC's of LIFE

YOU NOWHERE

JEALOUSY GETS YOU NOWHERE
{Jj}

Throughout school you mastered the concept of being jealous. Jealous of her hair. Jealous of his skills on the field. Jealous of her because she dates the boy you like. Jealous of him because he gets all the digits. Jealous of their life. Well, the reality is this – jealously gets you nowhere because you must justify your actions.

At some point, you need to stop being a "hater." You know these kinds of people. Haters are the ones who always have something discouraging to say or comment negatively about everyone else. Stop spending your time and energy being jealous of someone else's life. Stop doing the comparison of the "haves" and "have nots." While you spend your energy wondering why you are a have not, you could have just as well been pursuing what you wanted to do. People who are busy unlocking the power of their life don't have time to be jealous. There is action to be taken and work to be done. Start being the most positive person you know. Embrace the concept of you and understand that no one can beat you at being you. Simply put, jealousy gets you nowhere.

[fig. 11]

{Kk}

KEEP ON KEEP

{Kk}

ABC's of LIFE

IN' ON

KEEP ON KEEPIN' ON
{Kk}

There will be times in life when it seems like you are ready to throw in the towel. You are ready to give up, give in and give out. Don't do it. In the poem by Langston Hughes, a mother tells her son about trials and tribulations he may encounter in life. She goes on to tell him that out of everything that comes his way, not to sit and rest because he's got work to do. The mother says, "Keep on movin', reachin' landin's and turnin' corners, often going in the dark where there ain't been no light."

I don't know your situation or your circumstance, but I do know you didn't come this far to stop. My ultimate goal is to ascend above the clouds and I truly understand you cannot "sit" your way into heaven. In fact, you cannot be progressive by sitting your way anywhere. You have to keep on keepin' on and you may even have to kick some of those negative folks and negative habits to the curb.

If you truly desire to be highly successful, there will be people and things you'll have to say no to. It doesn't mean you are being condescending or looking down upon people, you simply realize that you are at a different place in life. Only you know what it will take for you to make it—so you must keep on keepin' on!

[fig. 12]

{L1}

LEARN HOW

L

ABC's OF LIFE

TO LEARN

LEARN HOW TO LEARN
{ L1 }

As a child, I was always told to learn something new everyday. Each and every morning that I would prepare to go to school, my mother would say "learn something new today." At the end of the day, mom would do a status check - "what did you learn new today?" I quickly learned that "nothing" was far from the right answer.

If you went to school, work or church for roughly 7-9 hours and you cannot explain or quantify what you learned, something is terribly wrong. With all of my education, I have spent approximately 22 years enrolled in formal school. In these cases I strived to give it my all because you only get out what you put in.

I profess to be a lifelong learner. This does not mean I plan to be enrolled in school for the rest of my life. However, I do understand with 100% certainty that the world is steadily changing. In order to be effective, I have to continue to learn, grow and prosper each and every day. I was told once that learning seemed too much like work. Call it what you want to, I caution you to never underestimate the importance of learning…formal or informal, street or otherwise. Learning is critical to your success as you go forward. The people who get passed by are the ones who stop learning how to learn.

[fig. 13]

{Mm}

MO' MONEY,
MO'

ABC's OF LIFE

MO' MONEY,
MONEY

MO' MONEY, MO' MONEY, MO' MONEY
{ M m }

Some time ago, a great musician decided to pen the words to a song – Mo' Money, Mo' Money, Mo' Money. Interesting enough, years later another songwriter revised those lyrics to be "Mo' Money, Mo' Problems." I jokingly tell people that I speak two languages – money and English. If you'd like to speak French let's discuss francs, if you'd like to speak Spanish, let's discuss pesos and if you want to speak Ebonics then let's begin with the "benjamins." Money is right up there with oxygen. You cannot live, breathe or die without it.

I contend that you should find something in life that you love doing, you'd do it for free – but do it so well you get paid for it. Thus it becomes an issue of mission over money and often if you are on target with your mission, the money will follow. Before you get it twisted, recognize that some careers offer better compensation while others offer peace of mind. If you decide to be an artist, know the majority of the money may not come until you are dead and buried.

Moreover, money should not be your master. You should measure your worth based upon what's inside your head and heart, not what's parked in your driveway or hanging in your closet. Live your life on purpose – concentrating on the mission, not the money.

[fig. 14]

{Nn}

NEVER, NEV

SAY

ABC's of LIFE

ER, NEVER
NEVER

NEVER, NEVER, NEVER
SAY NEVER
{N n}

When I was in college, it was popular to ask people what they would or would not do for money. Though I have yet to do anything out of the norm, the reality is unless you are exiting the earth in the next few minutes, you cannot truly say what you will or will not do. I do believe you have to live a life of principle. But as I speak of never, never, never say never – I'm referring to having that natural instinct to rise in the midst of adversity, not taking no for an answer.

So many have failed to realize their dreams, not due to a lack of potential but a lack of determination and hope in the future reality.

Because this is your life, you have the right to plot, plan and strategize on your future. Do not accept no for an answer, and never, never, never say never.

[fig. 15]

{Oo}

ORDER YOUR

100

ABC's of LIFE

STEPS

ORDER YOUR STEPS
{ O o }

As a strong person of faith, I utilize gospel music as a vehicle to help me transcend the world within which I live. One song that has encouraged me is entitled "Order My Steps." This song has always had a humbling effect at the very core of who I claim to be. I am reminded that it's by God's grace that I am who I am. For nothing I have achieved or attained was gained by my effort but rather through the wisdom, gifts and talents I've been blessed with in my life.

At some point you must recognize that the world is larger than you and a higher power guides all that you do. I hope that you pray daily, seeking wisdom and guidance for your steps to be ordered that you might fulfill the destiny awaiting you. Strive for meaning in your life. Understand that there is a divine design for your life. Whether you like it or not, you are designed to be a contribution.

> *"Order my steps in your word dear Lord.*
> *Lead me, guide me, everyday!*
> *Send your anointing, father I pray,*
> *Please order my steps in your word!"*

[fig. 16]

{Pp}
PRACTICE WHAT

ABC's OF LIFE

YOU PREACH

PRACTICE WHAT YOU PREACH

{ P p }

During my tenure as a school principal, I learned the value of "walking the walk and talking the talk." Children have this amazing ability to remind us that we, too, have expectations to live up to. It's one thing to set, establish or identify a model for others to live by. It is completely another to actually live that life. My elders in church referred to this as living the life you sing about. Of course that was before 50 Cent and Lil' Kim came on the scene.

The fact of the matter is you should spend more time practicing than preaching. In other words, most of your time should be spent doing, not telling. Instead of always trying to correct others, telling someone how to be a better person, your rubber should be meeting the road.

You should be living by the same high standards you require others to live by. You should understand that a person of character is one who does the right thing when no one else is looking. A person of high self-worth embraces the Golden Rule - treating others better than they'd like to be treated. Practice what you preach—let your actions speak for themselves.

[fig. 17]

{Qq}

QUIT QUIT

ABC's of LIFE

TING

QUIT QUITTING
{Q q}

Quit quitting! Quitters never win and winners never quit. We live in a society where you can take medication for almost anything you can imagine. I wish there was a medicine to force you to stick to your dreams and hold fast to your future, but it's yet to be invented. I meet so many people who become discouraged to the extent that they begin giving up in life. The sparkle and smile that used to highlight their face has been replaced with a frown and complete frustration.

My friend, you have to believe and understand that you can

never win if you quit. You are just getting started. While success may not come over night, it does come over time. You can never imagine the number of great successes throughout history who were on the verge of throwing in the towel. Yet, they achieved greatness because they never quit. I'm not saying it will not be tough or difficult. It will. It's during those times when it seems the world (including your family) has turned its back on you that you have to stay the course, knowing that this temporary setback is the only thing standing between you and achievement.

Dig in, suck it up and get your butt in gear. Great things are already in motion, awaiting your arrival. Don't you dare quit; you've come this far to make it.

[fig. 18]

{Rr}

RESPECT

{Rr}

ABC's of LIFE

PEOPLE

RESPECT PEOPLE

{R r}

The issue of respect is central to leadership and success in life. Some believe you command respect while others believe you demand it. The reality is this…just because you have a title and people respond to your title doesn't mean they respect you. It's doesn't even mean they respect the title you have or the position you hold.

You should become a person who earns respect as well as you give it. I have encountered people from all walks of life. Those who have come from "losing lane" to "luxury avenue" and from "luxury avenue" to "losing lane." In the final analysis, I respect people based upon their skills, talents and achievements and nothing else.

No matter your vocation or avocation, you should desire to be a person who is respected by those with whom you live, work and play. I will be the first to say that I'm not usually concerned with whether people like me or not as long as they respect me. An excellent leader is liked and well respected. You have the ability to achieve both, especially when you remember that you have to bring some respect to get some respect – when and where it is due.

[fig. 19]

{ Ss }

STAY STRONG
VALUES

ABC's of LIFE

TO YOUR
AND BELIEFS

STAY STRONG TO YOUR
VALUES AND BELIEFS

{ Ss }

Society advances at such a rapid rate, I'm amazed people are able to keep up. It's so easy and convenient to follow the latest trend or adopt the current slang of your day. I would caution you not to get so caught up with the "here and now" that you forget about the "there and then."

A key to success in life is staying strong to your core values and beliefs. You have to stay true to those principles, which guide what you do and govern who you are in life. I read a quote once, which said,

"What is popular is not always right and what is right, is not always popular."

I hope you have an internal compass, which provides direction for your life. When you are in the midst of difficult times when you might consider selling out or compromising your beliefs, it's that internal compass which says, "there is danger ahead." Every morning the sun rises, you have to look yourself in the mirror and determine whether you are happy with whom you are and the person you are becoming.

Should you stay strong to your values and beliefs, you'll find that in spite of your situation or circumstance, you can smile at the person you see in the mirror and say good morning without feeling ashamed or guilty for anything. Stay true to your values and beliefs – they will serve you well if you live by them!

[fig. 20]

{Tt}

TRAVEL THE
TO

ABC's OF LIFE

LONG ROAD
EQUALITY

TRAVEL THE LONG ROAD
TO EQUALITY
{ T t }

Many would like to think that society is now a level playing field. I have traveled extensively across the United States and around the globe and have discovered this simply is not the case. Whether it is gender, religion, intelligence, age, weight, sexual preference, socio-economic or any other classification – the world in which we live is not an equal place.

You need to recognize and move forward. Don't get caught up on the conversation of the "haves" and "have nots." While this is very important, the time you spend justifying your situation could just as well be spent moving from point A to Z. I'm not saying disregard the inequalities in life, but rather acknowledge them for what they are and prepare to move forward in the midst of adversity.

People will hate on you no matter what you do, who you are or where you are from. How you respond to the "hateration" (to borrow a word from Mary J. Blige) is what's of vital significance. I refuse to allow someone else to define who I am or limit where I can go. I'm just not gonna do it. Thus, the road to equality is long and hard…so what else is new. What are you gonna do – stop? I think not; instead enjoy the thrill of the ride to victory. How sweet it will be!

[fig. 21]

{Uu}

UTILIZE YOUR

ABC's of LIFE

NETWORK

UTILIZE YOUR NETWORK
{Uu}

Never underestimate the value of networking. I attribute a significant portion of my success to the value of a network. While you may not personally have an outstanding network as of yet, don't hesitate to seek a mentor or advisor and tap into their network.

As a student in high school and undergrad, I was very involved in Junior Achievement. After completing a summer internship, I maintained contact with people whom I encountered from the national staff. One of my key advisors right now (Evelyn) agreed to mentor me during my participation. Evelyn would position me to take advantage of great opportunities. Though I may not have understood the value or purpose, she would make sure I was ready and prepared to excel in the environment.

From that network, I established a network with celebrities, dignitaries, elected officials, and corporate executives. Evelyn and I have maintained contact through some 15 years now and we continue to access each other's network as needed.

There's an old saying "It's not what you know, it's who you know." Whose Rolodex are you in? Who is in your circle of influence? Your network should be full of contacts, direct and indirect. That great law of six degrees of separation is true. If you are doing what you should be doing, you are only six degrees away from any person or anything you need access to—utilize your network.

[fig. 22]

{Vv}

VISUALIZE

IT

ABC's of LIFE

VISUALIZE IT

{V v}

Only when you see it, can you be it. The ability to be a visionary is a powerful tool. I consider it one of the greatest keys to success, yet one of the least talked about. You have to be able to not only create a vision for your life but also be able to articulate and enroll others in that vision.

When I started Progressive Schools, I could tell you what the classroom, cafeteria, staff, students and buses looked liked. Though I could not physically show others, I could certainly share the vision verbally and enroll them in the concept to ensure its success.

How do you know what success looks like when you attain it? You have to have some indication within your mind and heart about the vision for your life. The Word says, "Write the vision and make it plain that men may read it and run with it!" It also says, "Without vision, the people perish."

You'll be surprised at how motivated you become and your ability to inspire others when you can see it all unfold before your very eyes…live, in living color. Visualize it! Only when you see it, can you be it.

[fig. 23]

{Ww}

WORK, WORK, YOUR WORK

{Ww}

ABC's of LIFE

WORK - 'TIL
IS DONE

WORK, WORK, WORK - 'TIL YOUR WORK IS DONE
{ W w }

Not sure if I've mentioned it along the way but your success depends on your willingness to actually do the work. This may mean getting your hands dirty or breaking a sweat. Whatever it takes to get the job done. You have to be willing to do the work. I know you may think other people should drop what they are doing and begin to help you with your work.

Well, it doesn't quite work that way. For some strange reason, people don't get involved with the great work you're doing until they realize it's a success in the making. Thus, you can't count on others to do your work. If they pitch in and help out – great; but if they don't, your show will still be going strong.

All of the ventures I've pursued (business and advanced education) required that I work twice as hard and twice as long as others. You have to be willing to do today, what other's won't do – to have tomorrow what others never will. In short, you have to be willing to do the work. Just as there is no shortcut to greatness, there is no shortcut to getting the job done.

[fig. 24]

{Xx}

X-RAY YOUR

ABC's of LIFE

OWN LIFE

X-RAY YOUR OWN LIFE

$\{Xx\}$

Many people spend their lives on the verge of success. Getting to where you want to be can be as simple as minding and tending to your own business. Instead of analyzing the lives of others (what they have, their motivations, etc.) you should be x-raying your own life for improvement.

As a student and a school administrator, I quickly discovered that the students who were in trouble most frequently were those who could not and would not tend to their own business. It's human nature to be curious and inquisitive. Given the dreams you have, all of your time should be spent inquiring about how to make them come true. Otherwise you'll be like most, sitting on the sidelines of life waiting to get into the game.

In essence, you have 24 hours in a day- 12 hours to mind your business and 12 hours to take care of your business, which leaves ZERO time for anybody else's business. The game has already started, get with the program and X-ray your own life.

[fig. 25]

{Yy}

YIELD TO OPP

ABC's OF LIFE

Yy

ORTUNITY

YIELD TO OPPORTUNITY
{ Y y }

Occasionally, I find myself rushing from one project or activity to another before completing the first. In the midst of my haste, I may miss significant opportunities staring me right in the face. While I encourage your enthusiasm for success and life in general, remember to allow time to take advantage of what life has to offer in the present.

I have to remind myself to slow down and enjoy the ride, allowing time for great things to happen along the way. It's one thing to mentally recognize you need to yield to opportunity; it's another to physically do it.

As you structure your life plan, know that you will encounter detours along the highway of success. These may take you five days out of your way to accomplish your goals or you may spend five years heading in a slightly different direction with your eyes still fixed upon the prize. There is no right or wrong. Life often surprises us with some of the most beautiful blessings when we yield to opportunity.

It's like that great expression; take time to stop and smell the roses. If your life is so carefully planned and executed you may not have the time to follow up or take advantage of a wonderful opportunity. It may initially seem like it takes you off course, but it more than likely will only propel you further into the future. YIELD, I say, YIELD!

[fig. 26]

{Zz}

ZEALOUSLY STR

{ Zz }

ABC'S of LIFE

IVE TO ACHIEVE

ZEALOUSLY STRIVE TO ACHIEVE
{ Z z }

When it comes to your life, I wish you passion, patience and personal power as you strive to achieve. In order to do this and place the 25 other keys in perspective…you must zealously strive to achieve.

With every fiber of your being, you have to know that you have what it takes to make it. You should be zealous in all that you do. Pursue your dreams like a child let loose in a candy store; not knowing when your mother will say it's time to go, so you get all you can while you can.

You are destined for great things and your future is growing brighter by the second. Allow tenacity to be your fuel, passion to be your engine, and your zeal to be the oil that keeps the motor running. With everything within you, zealously strive to achieve and you will live a prosperous life.

ABC's OF LIFE

ABOUT BYRON V. GARRETT

In June of 2008, Byron V. Garrett became the first male and 2nd African American Chief Executive Officer at the National Parent Teachers Association. PTA has over 5 million members and over 23,000 units across the country. A visionary leader, prior to joining PTA, Byron had a distinguished career in the government sector. Byron served as the first Chief of Staff for the Office of Public Affairs at the US Customs and Border Protection, an agency of the US Department of Homeland Security. Previously, Byron held a career appointment with the Cooperative State Research Education and Extension Service at USDA as National Program Leader for the National 4-H Headquarters in Washington, DC. In this capacity, Byron represented the agency on the Executive Committee of the Helping America's Youth Initiative, serving as Co-Convener of the Program Group producing six regional conferences. Byron was also instrumental in hosting the White House Conference on School Safety in follow up to the school shootings during the fall of 2006. Prior to relocating to Washington, DC, Byron served as an appointee in the administration of Arizona Governor, Janet Napolitano, where he served as Policy Advisor on Faith and

Community Initiatives and Director of the Governor's Division for Community and Youth Development.

A community leader and youth development advocate, Byron is the former Principal and Co-Founder of two charter schools: Progressive Leadership Academy and Progressive Junior High School. Both schools embrace the motto: "It's Better To Build Children, Than To Repair Men and Women."

An accomplished writer, Byron is a former columnist for the Arizona Informant, having interviewed celebrities including Vanessa Williams, Samuel Jackson, Jude Law, Rachel Wiesz, and Raven Symone. Byron is the author of four books and co-author of three others including the popular - *Lead Now or Step Aside* and *Go MAD: Make A Difference.*

A highly sought after speaker, trainer and leadership consultant, Byron continues to travel the globe speaking before audiences from 50 to over 50,000. With a passion for challenging thoughts, changing minds, and offering the courage to commit, Byron provides a very real message for real times.

PERSPECTIVES FROM LEADERS

"Byron Garrett is right on target with the ABC's of Life. I constantly refer youth, co-workers, friends and family to this book. Regardless of age, race or socio-economic background, The ABC's of Life will touch and inspire you."

Phil Clark, Coordinator, Red Ribbons Works

"Byron Garrett knows the ABC's of Life, because he's lived every letter to the extreme. His stories connect to the heart and his real world advice is as practical as it is timeless. This book is a must-read for young and old alike."

Eric Chester, President of Generation Why, and creator of the Teen Power/Lead Now book series

"The best and most lasting lessons in life are simple and powerful. That's why The ABC's of Life has helped thousands unlock their future. To live a life of purpose can be difficult, but when you know your ABC's it all becomes possible."

Cloves Campbell, Publisher of the Arizona Informant & President, West Coast Black Publishers Association

"Having worked with Byron for over a decade, The ABC's of Life are tried, true, and proven. His message transcends generational and cultural boundaries providing business leaders from all walks of life the keys to excel and achieve."

Jean Buckley, President & CEO, Future Business Leaders of America

"Byron has inspired thousands of our members through his ABC's of Life. His message has helped them unlock their potential in families, schools, and communities across America."

Alan Rains, Executive Director,
Family Career & Community Leaders of America

"Byron Garrett clearly demonstrates the true aspect of leadership that we are in need of today. He embraces Caring, Honesty, Respect and Responsibility as key components of his daily life. These are the core values the YMCA has lived up to for over 155 years. Byron is on to something!"

Pablo Munoz, National Board Member, YMCA USA

"The ABC's of Life provides practical knowledge to help you achieve the divine design for your life. It is a must have for any young adult or youth ministry."

Rev. Alexis Thomas, State Bishop,
Full Gospel Baptist Church Fellowship International

"Byron is a profound speaker/educator who is blessed with the ability to touch youth and adults with his encouraging and real messages. The definitions in his "ABC's" are a road map for life that helps to motivate and stimulate thought and action by making it plain for everyone to understand. I congratulate him on his book and the positive impact he is making in our community."

The Honorable Pamela C. Gutierrez, Justice of the Peace

"The ABC's of Life encapsulates Garrett's simple but thought provoking view of life. This may very well be one of the most reflective treaties of our time. Enjoy the immersion into this timeless wisdom."

Leonard Knight, National Board Member, 100 Black Men of America, Inc.

TO ORDER

If you would like to purchase additional copies of *The ABC's of Life*, please call or email:

spkr4life@lifeworks101.com
1.888.786.7526

For booking and speaking information,
or more great books, please visit
www.ByronGarrett.com